The Sky Bridge

Poems by Jill Eggleton
Illustrated by Ann Skelly

CONTENTS

The Sky Bridge	2
Worm	4
Fishing	5
The Wind	6
Apple from the Apple Tree	7
I Want a Cat	8
Catch a Star!	10
I Used to Be…	12
Laugh!	13
The Elephant Sneezed	14
The Hippo	16
Moon in the Sky	18
Night Shadows	20
Bird Party	22
Crocodile Creek	24

Rigby

The Sky Bridge

The rainbow is
a sky bridge
stretching
over the sky.
But you cannot
climb the sky bridge
no matter how you try.

You cannot climb
the sky bridge,
for no one,
no one, knows
where the
sky bridge starts
and where the
sky bridge goes.

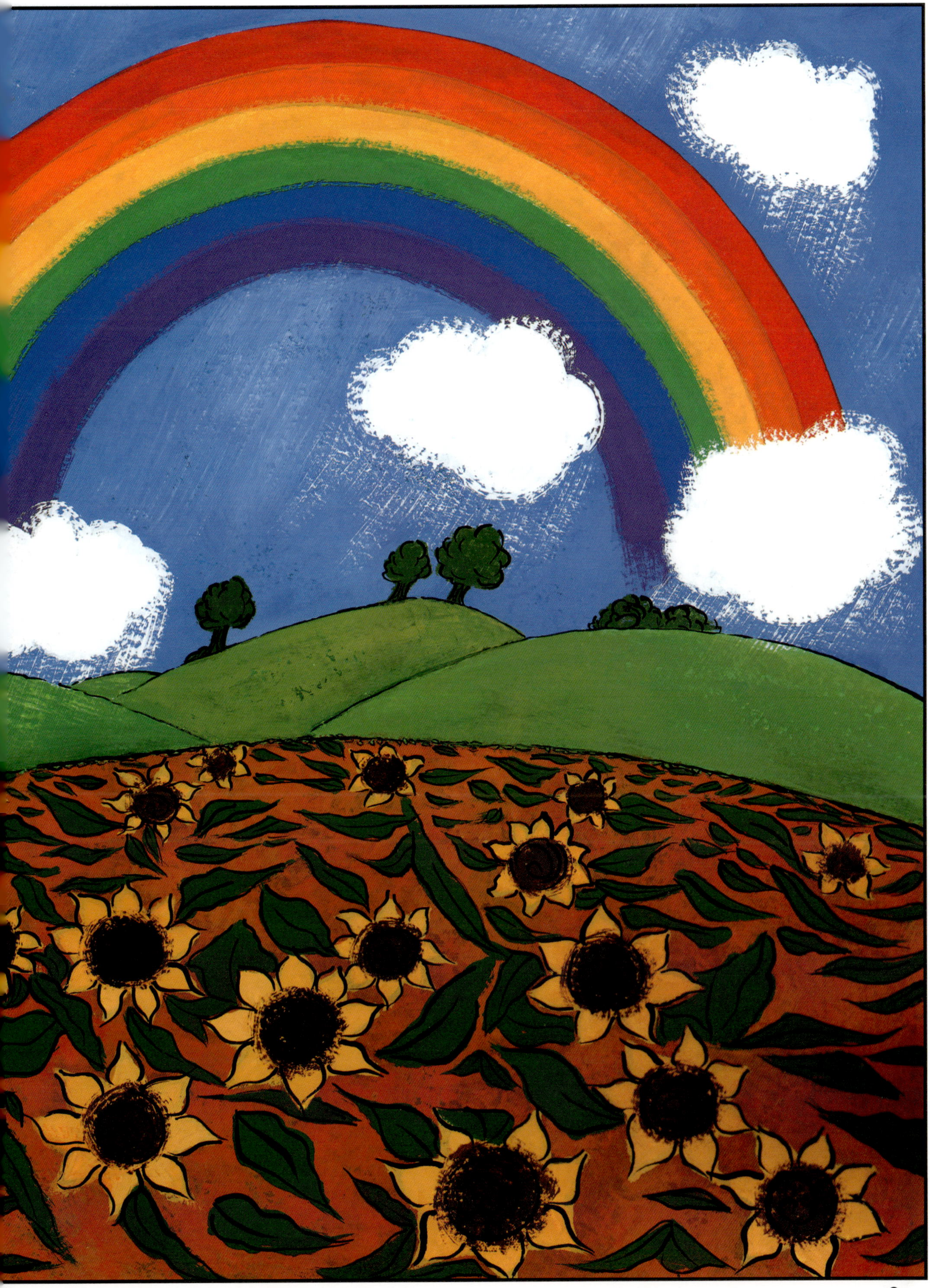

Worm

I wouldn't like
to be a worm.
It wouldn't be much fun,
hiding from the birds
and hiding from the sun.

I wouldn't like
to be a worm
and only squirm around,
eating leaves and dirt
and living underground.

Fishing

I caught a fish
on my fishing line.
"This fish," I said,
"is mine, mine, mine!"

But it wriggled,
and it wriggled,
till it wriggled free
and it swam
to the bottom
of the deep blue sea.

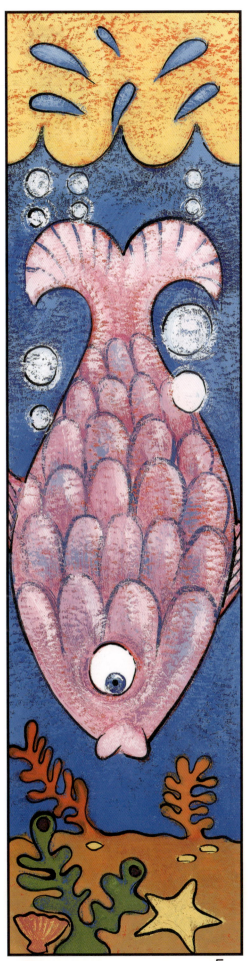

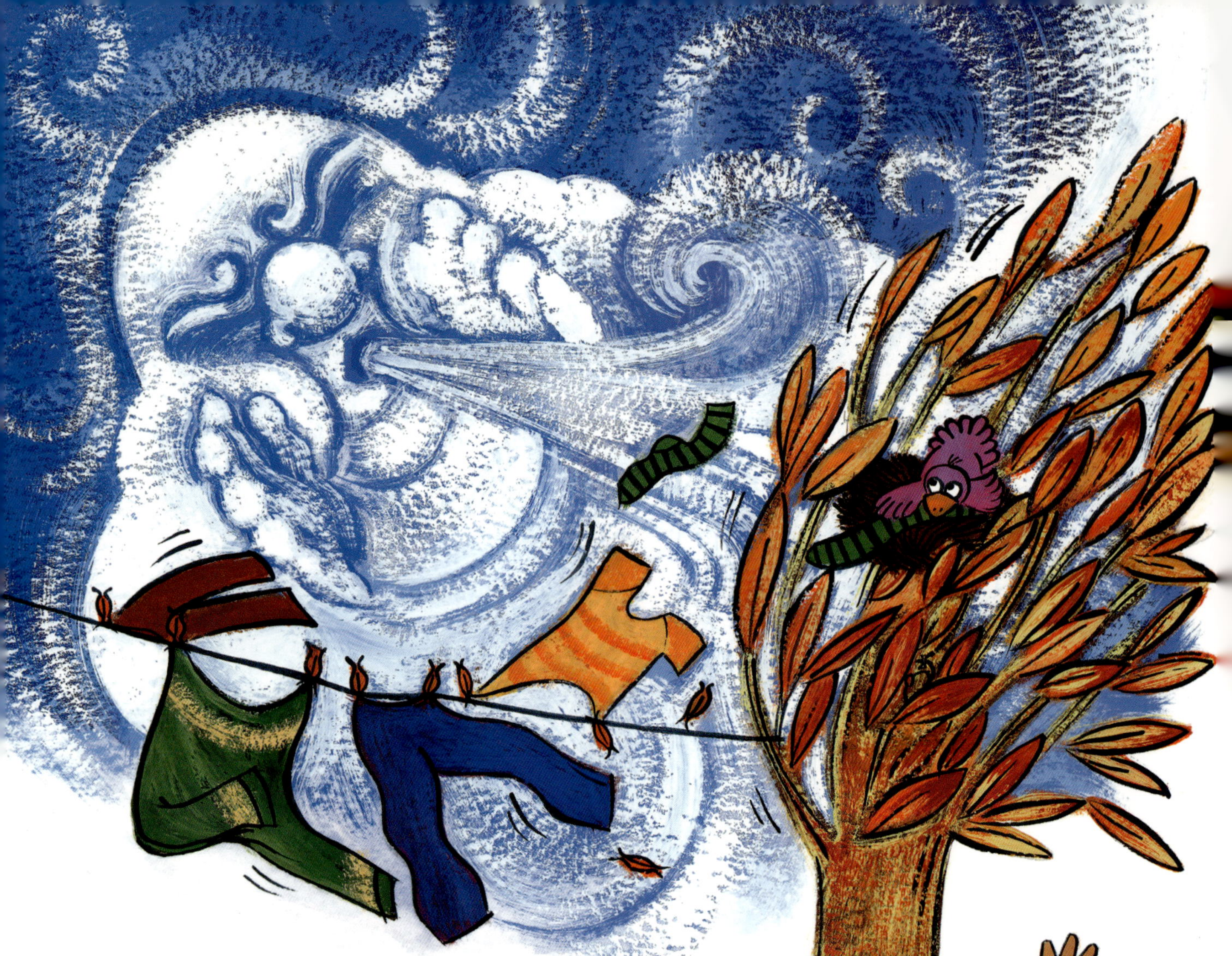

The Wind

“Stop, Mr. Wind,
those socks are mine!
Please leave my socks
on the clothesline!”

But the wind didn’t stop
to listen to me.
It gave my socks
to a bird in a tree.

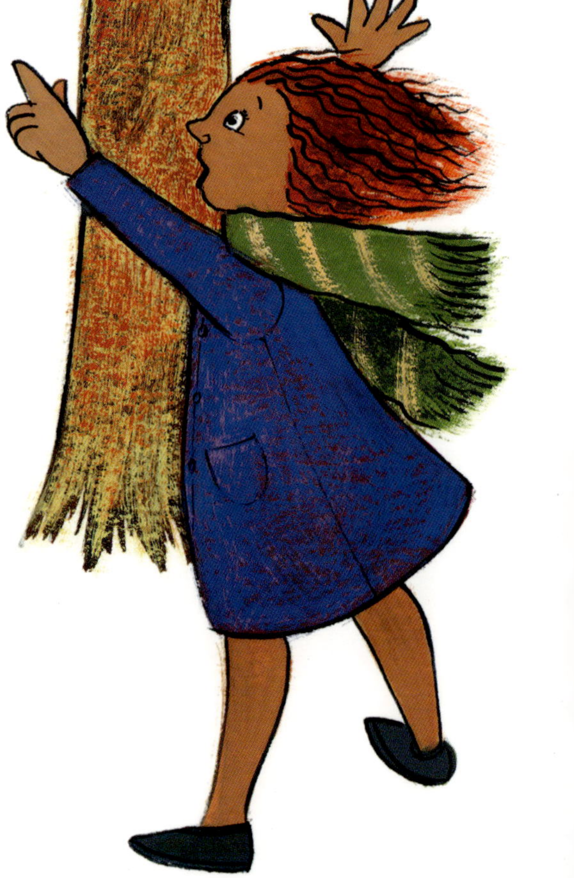

Apple from the Apple Tree

I got an apple
from the apple tree,
but the apple had a hole
and I didn't see.

I bit the apple
and it made me squirm,
for the apple had a hole,
and the hole had a worm!

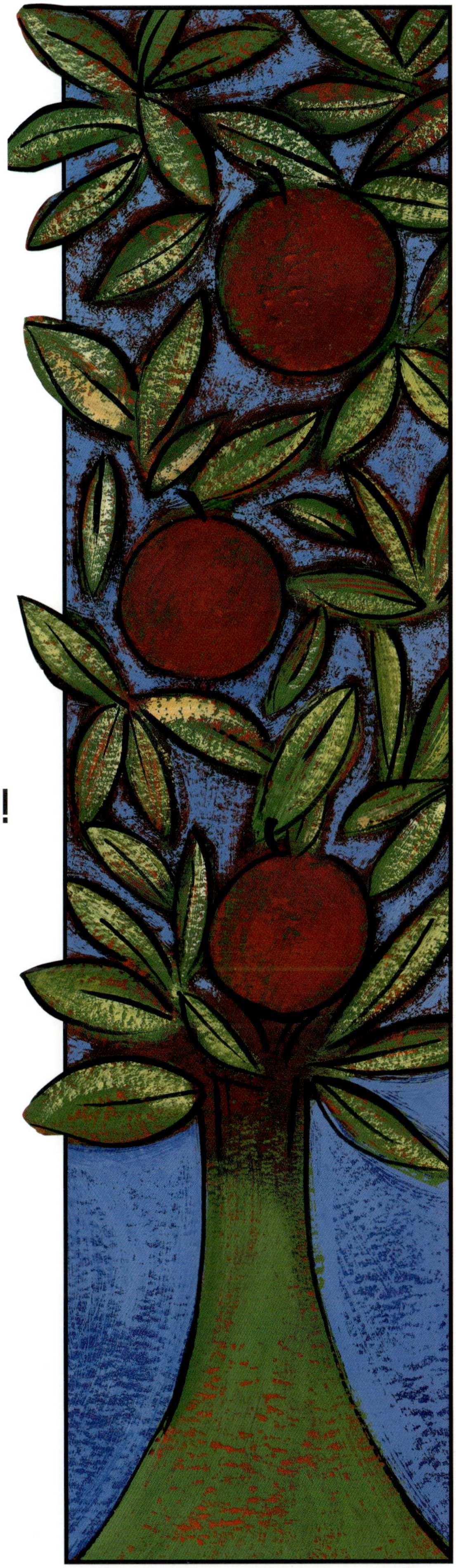

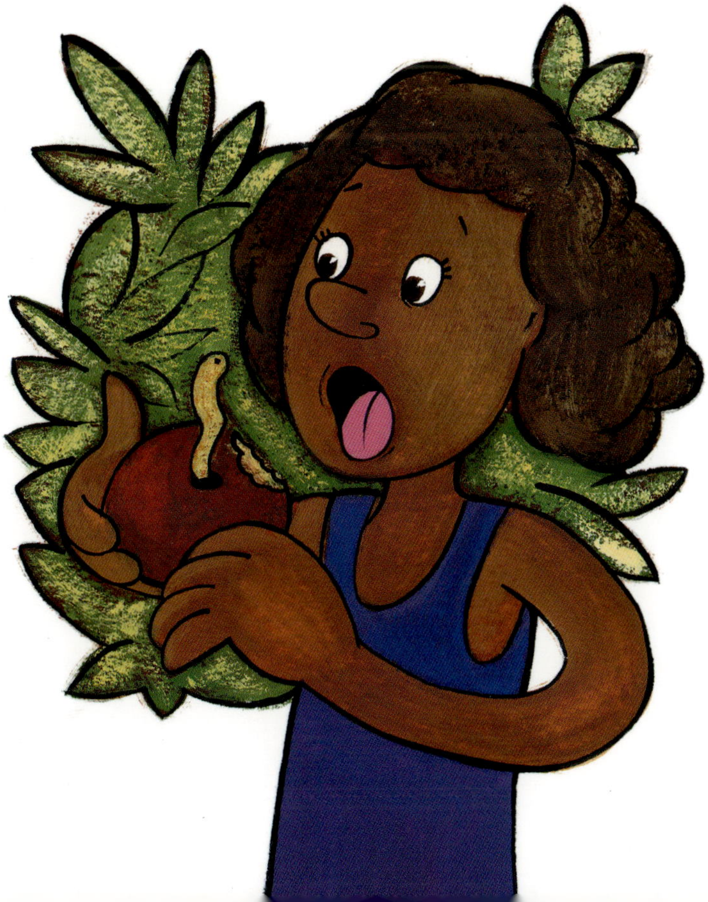

I Want a Cat

I want a cat!
I want one now,
but Mom said, "**no.**"

"Cats just meow.
Cats just sleep.
Cats just eat and
get under your feet!

Have a fish!"
my mom said.

But . . .
I can't take a fish
to bed!

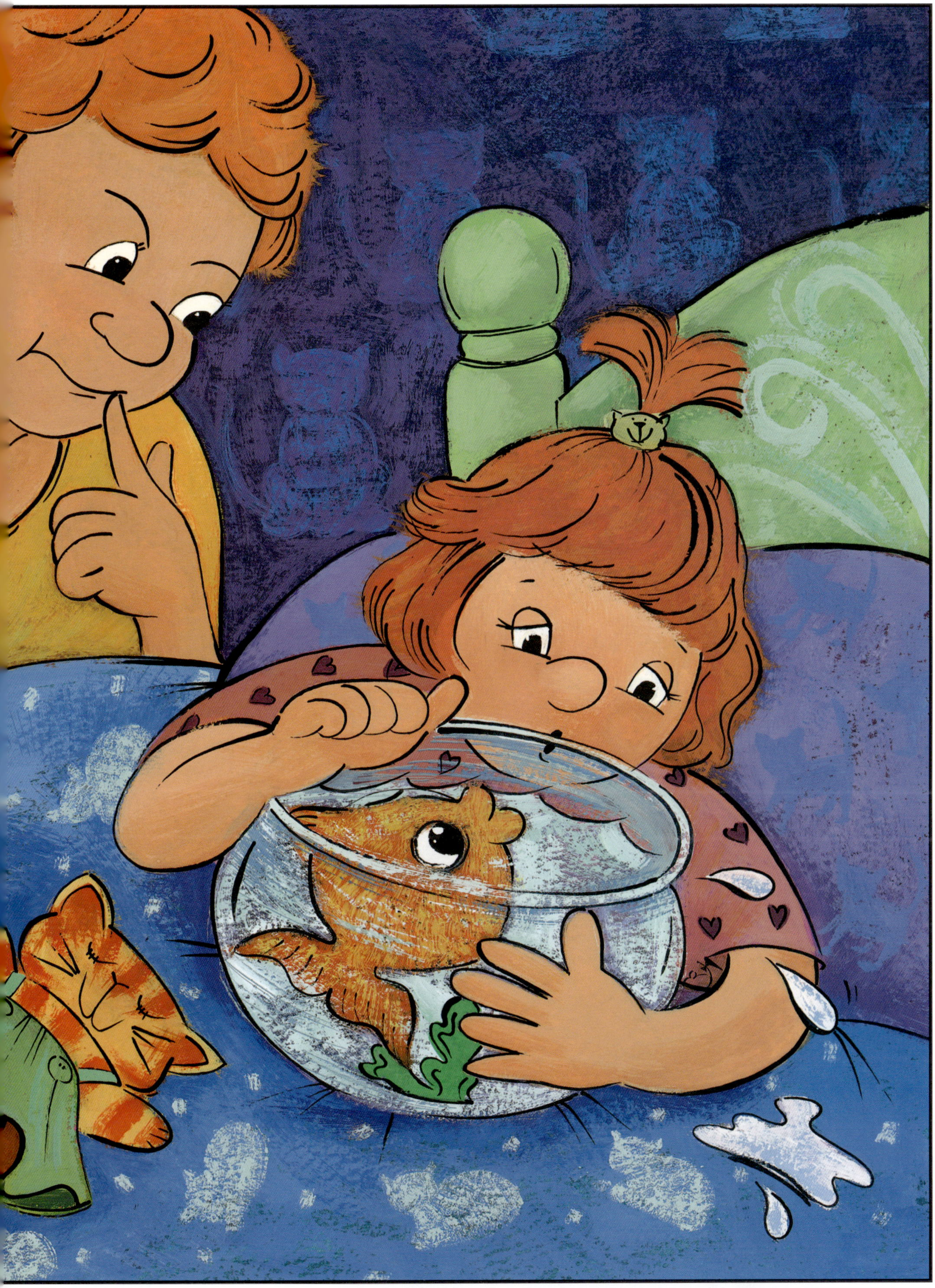

Catch a Star!

I would like
to catch a star
that twinkles in the sky.

I would like
to catch a star
but stars are way too high.

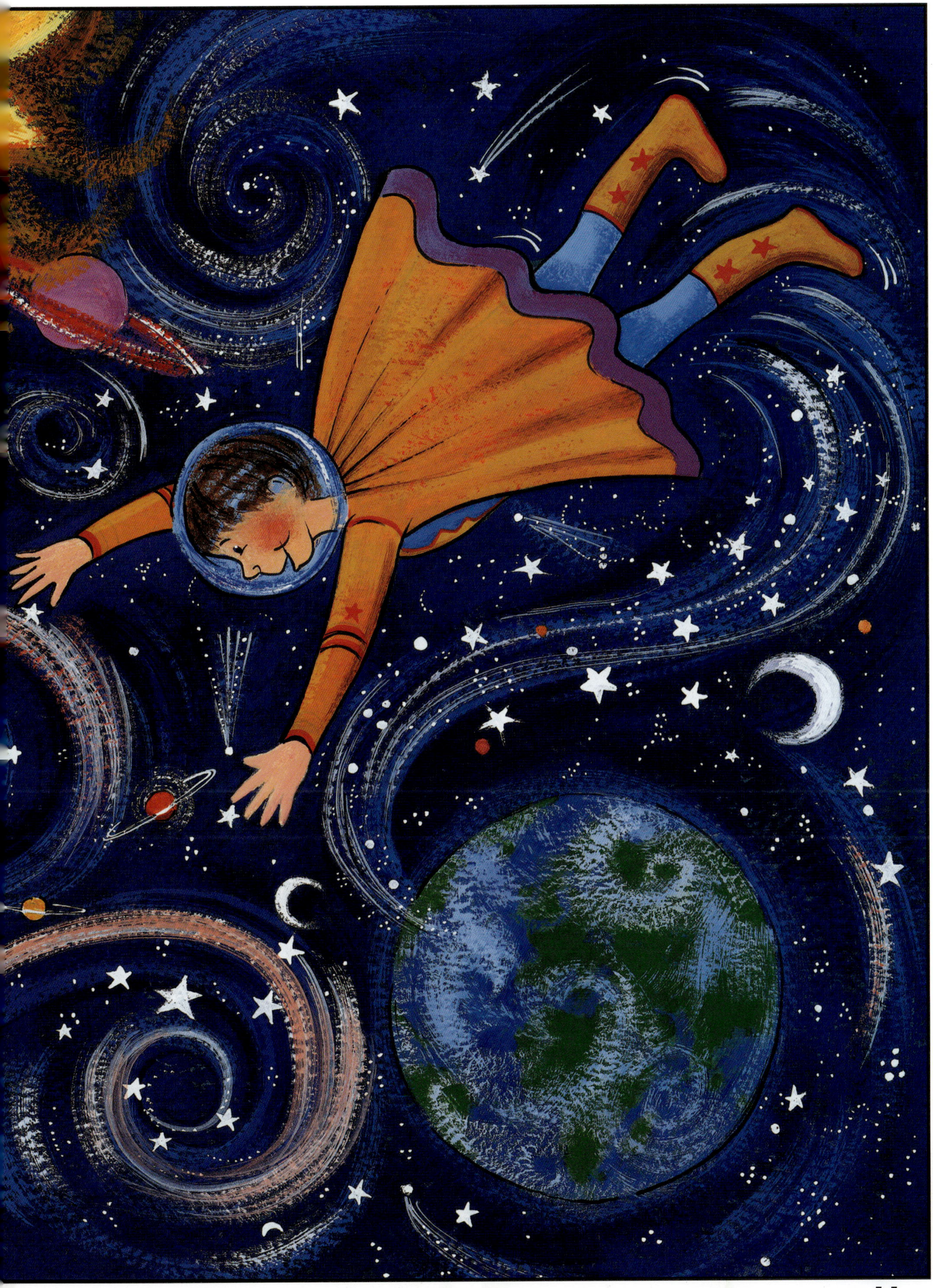

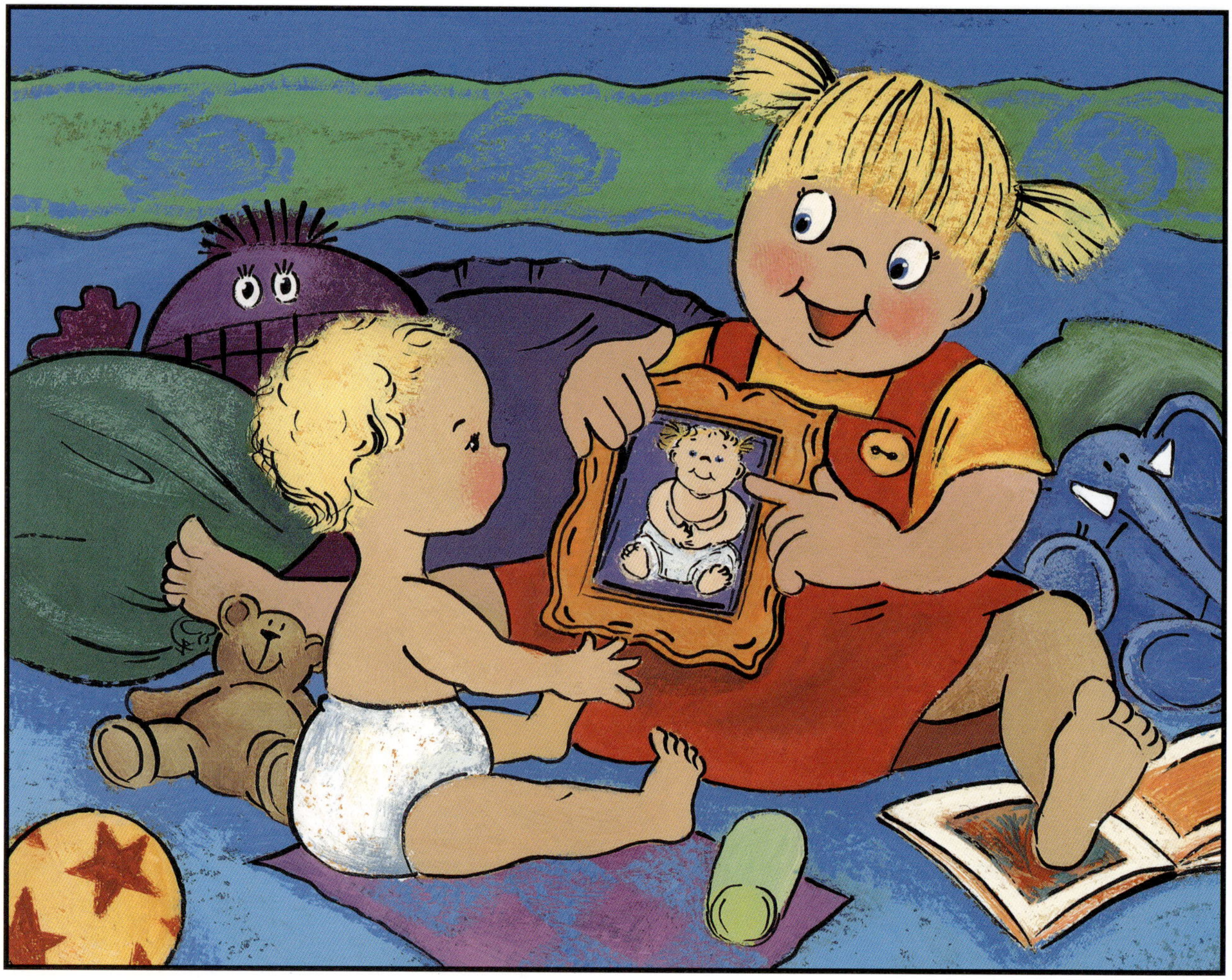

I Used to Be...

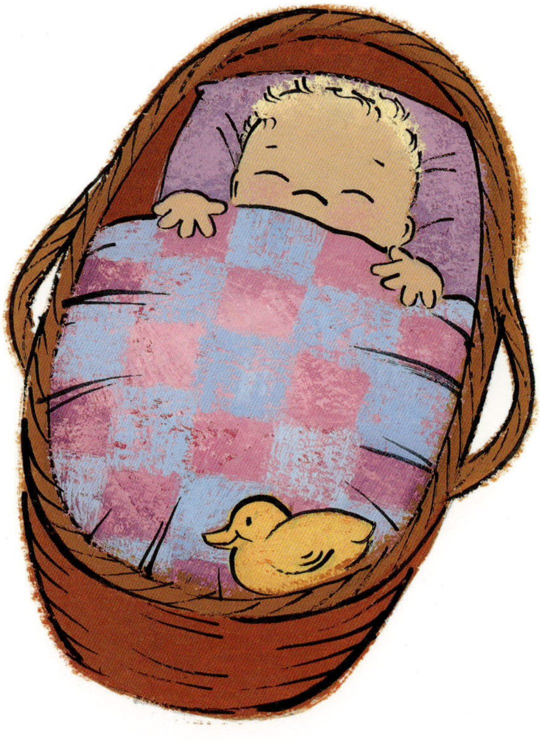

I used to be a baby
my mom said.
I used to wear diapers
in my bed.

I used to be a baby
and gurgle and goo.
I used to be a baby,
just like you!

Laugh!

"Laugh!"
said the giraffe.
So what did
the animals do?

They laughed so hard
that the fence fell down,
and they all ran
out of the zoo.

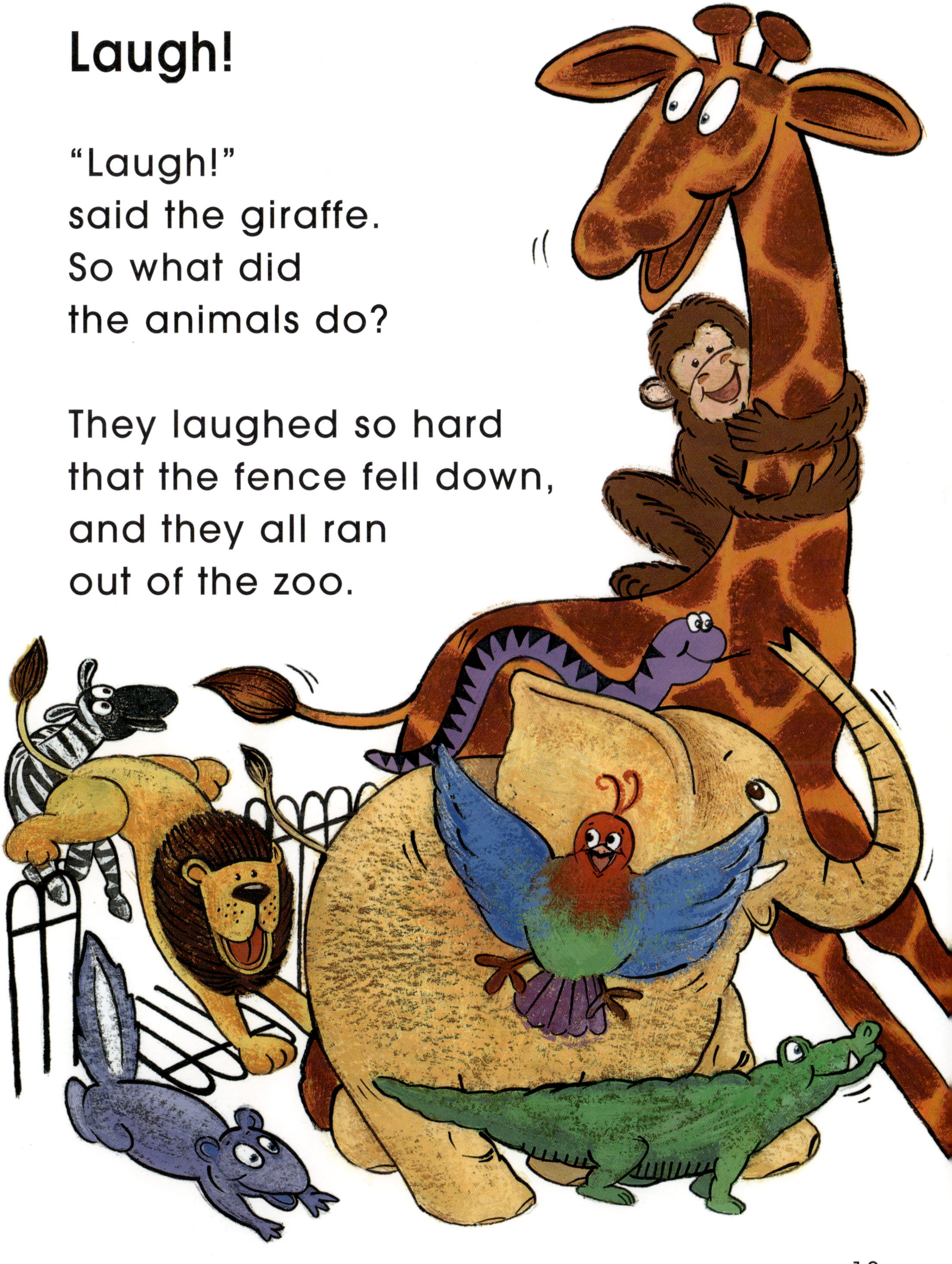

The Elephant Sneezed...

The elephant
sneezed a
humongous
sneeze!

It blew
the leaves
off the trees.

It made the bugs
and beetles fly.

And it blew
the clouds
right out
of the sky.

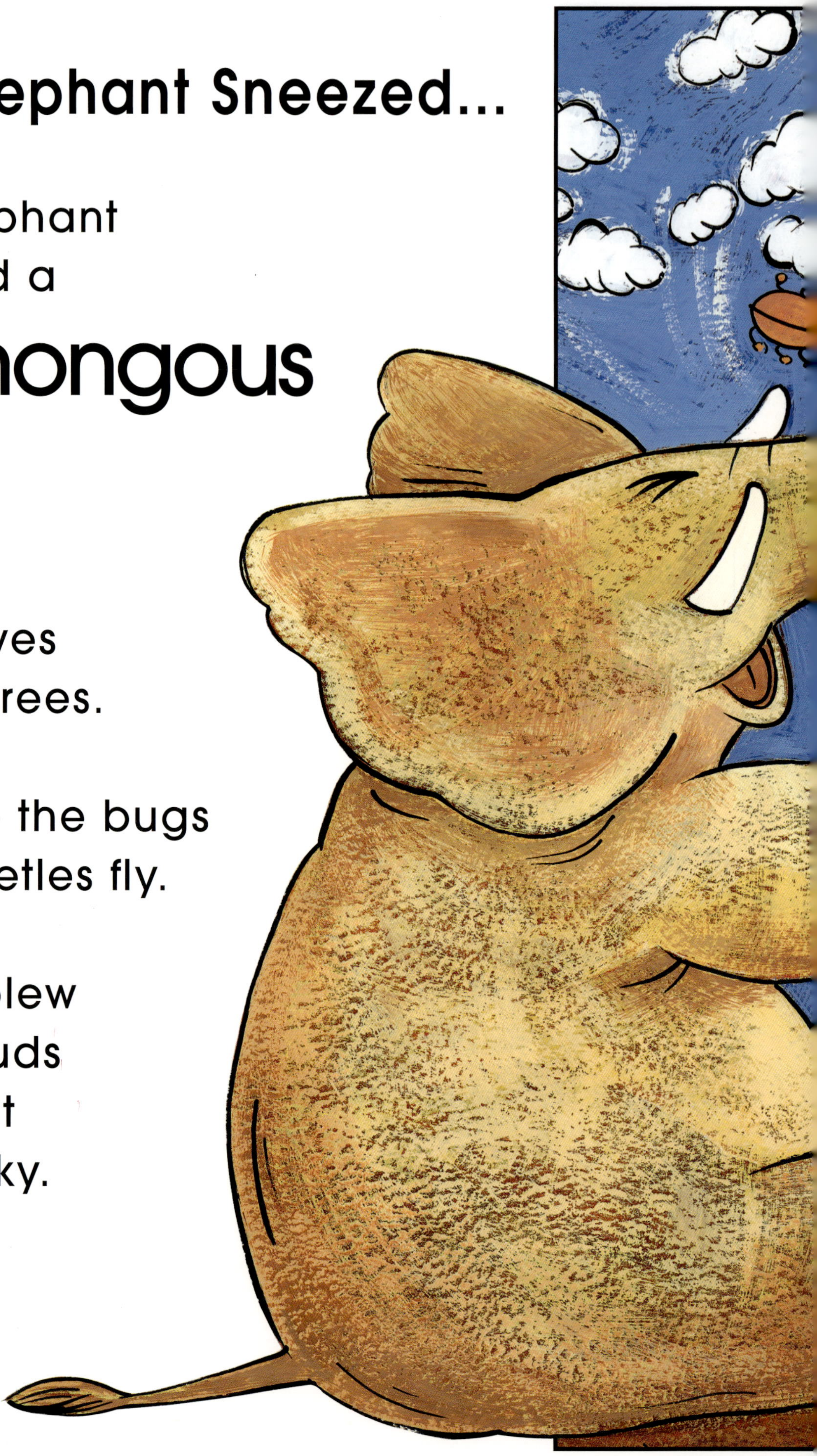

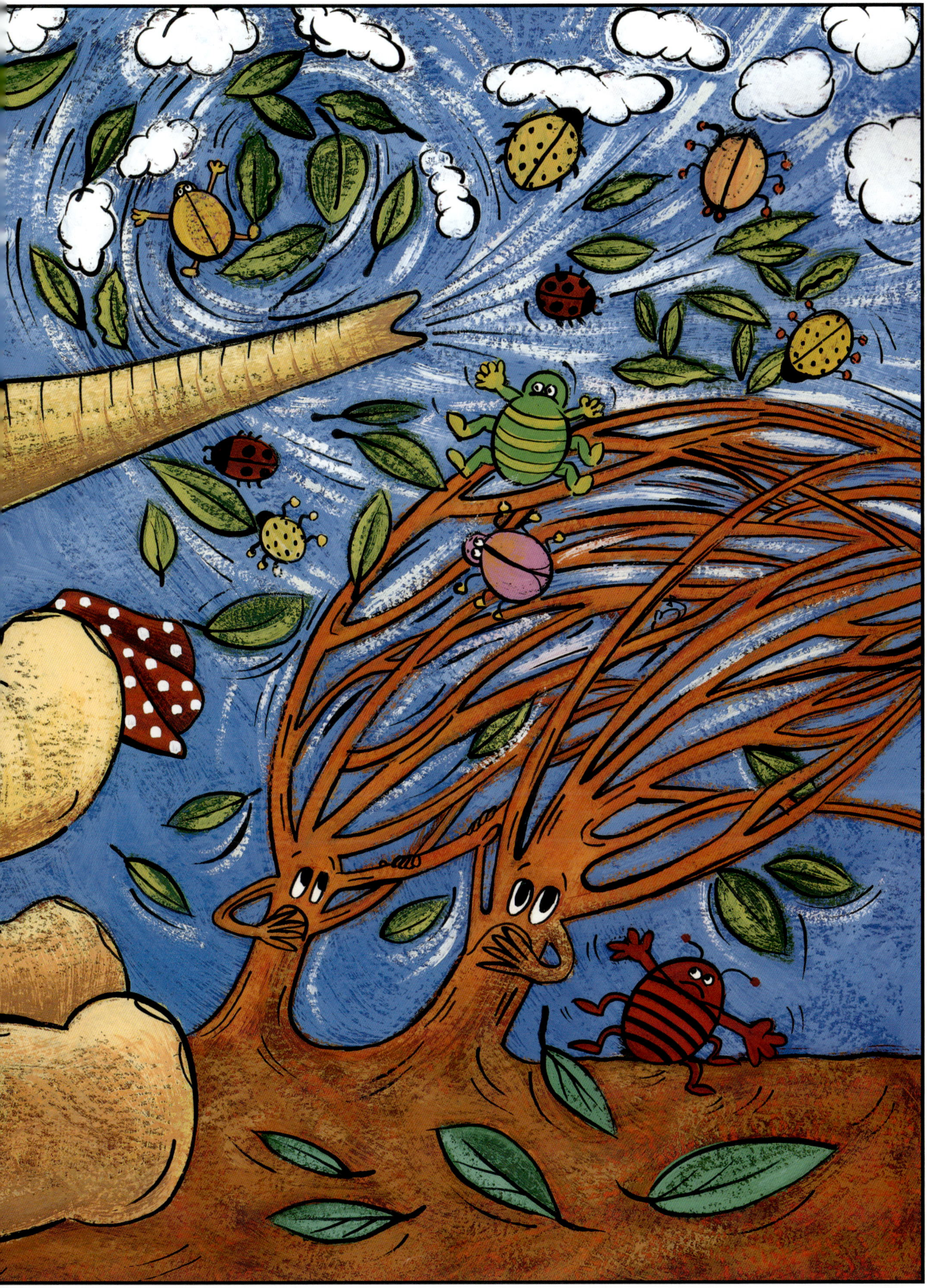

The Hippo

The hippo at the zoo
got thinner and thinner.
He wouldn't eat his lunch
and he wouldn't eat his dinner.

The doctor came
and the doctor said:
"Put that hippo into bed!
Get some socks
for his hippo feet
and give him
chocolate cake to eat!"

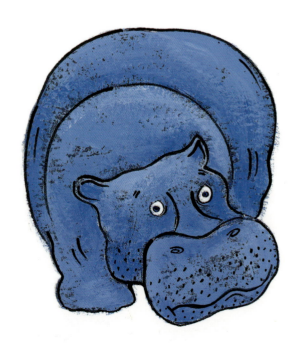

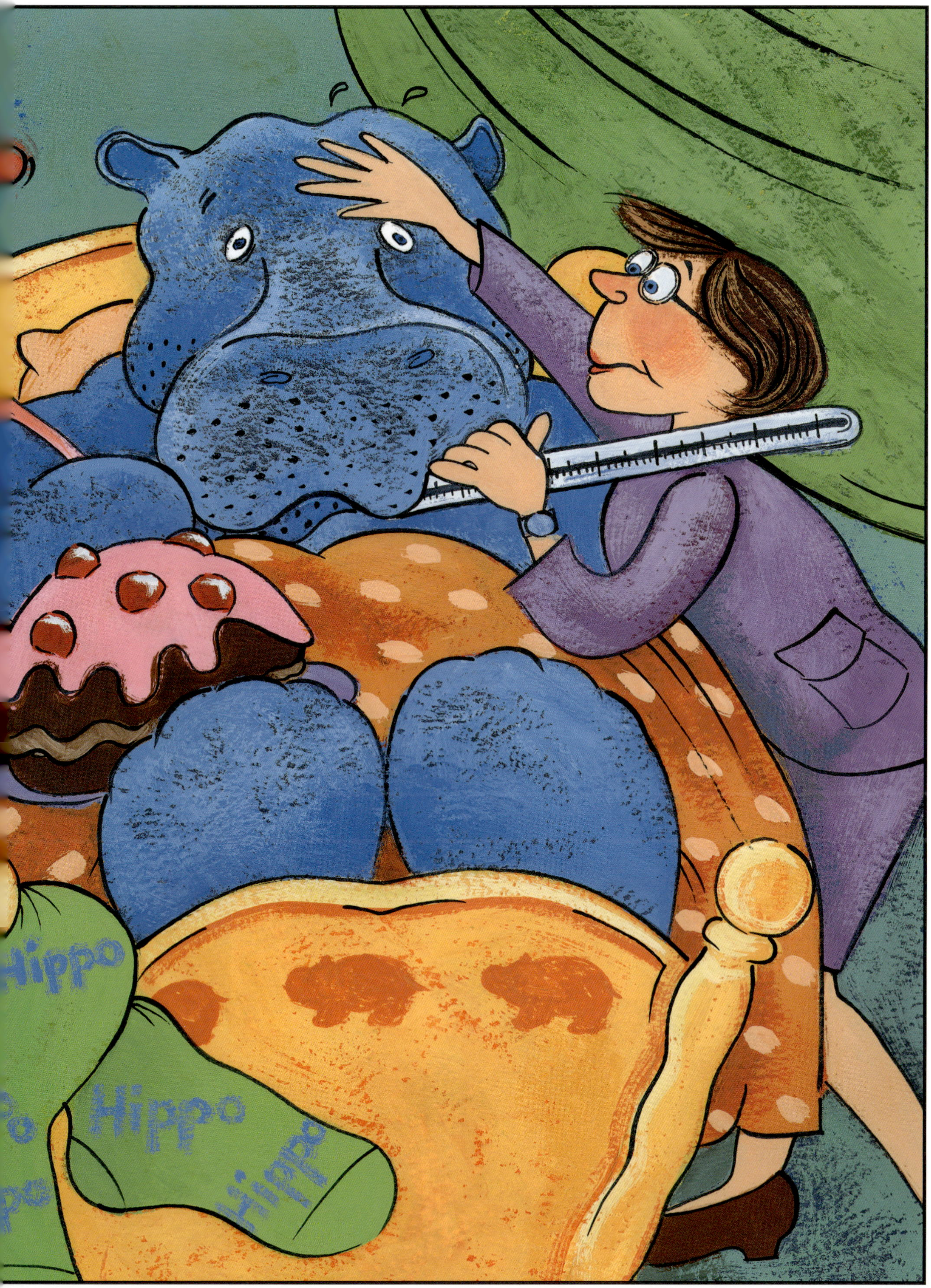
Hippo
Hippo
Hippo

Moon in the Sky

I look at the moon
in the sky at night.
I look at the moon,
when it's big and bright.

I look at the moon,
when it's round like a ball,
And I say to the moon,
"Never, ever fall!
If you fell from the sky,
it would be a mistake,
for what a horrible hole
you would make!"

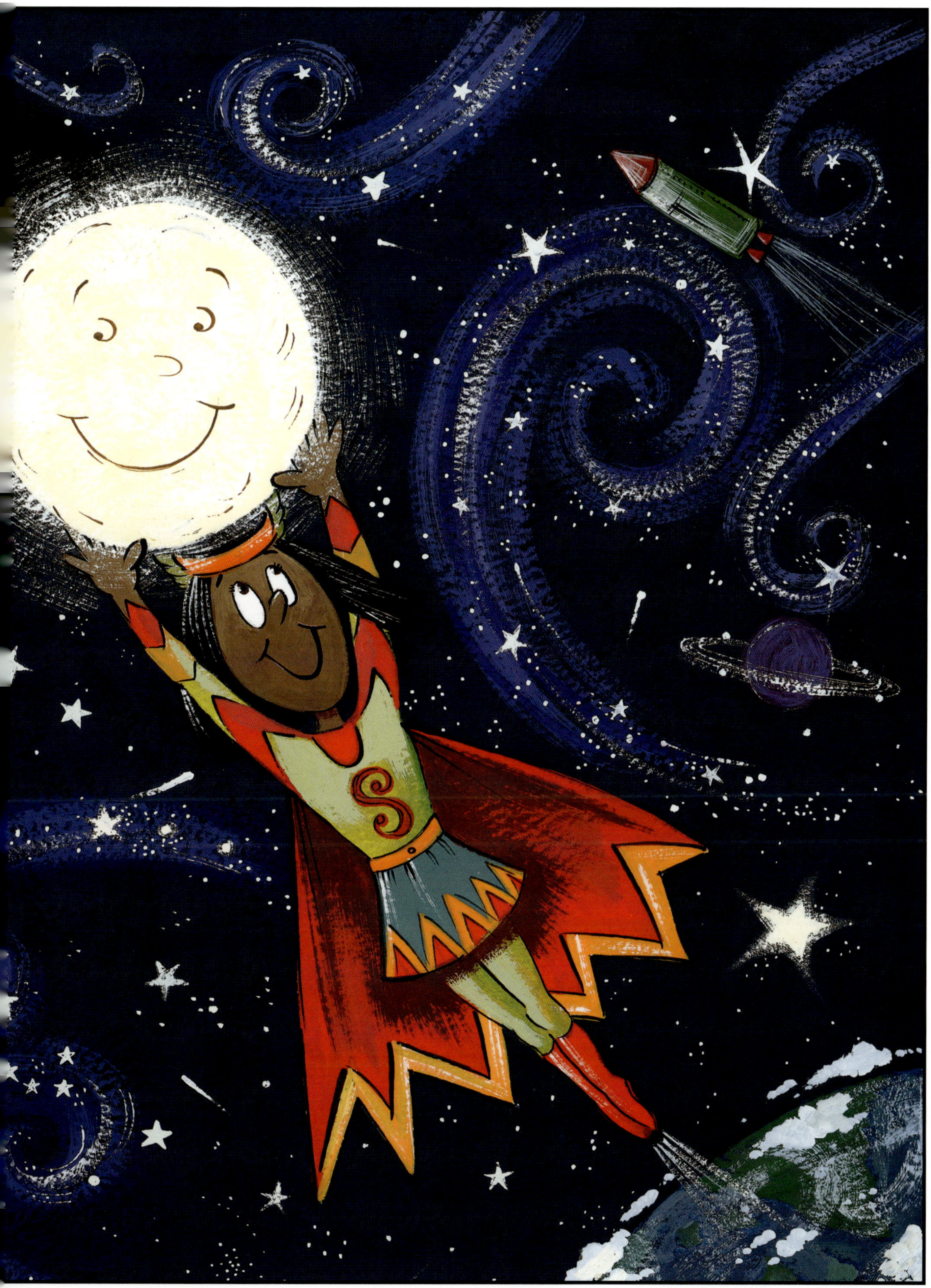
S

Night Shadows

At night, there are shadows
that dance on the wall.
Some shadows are big.
Some shadows are small.

They dance on the ceiling.
They dance on the floor.
They dance on the curtains.
They dance on the door.

At night there are shadows,
but when it is day,
the shadows, I know,
will go dancing away.

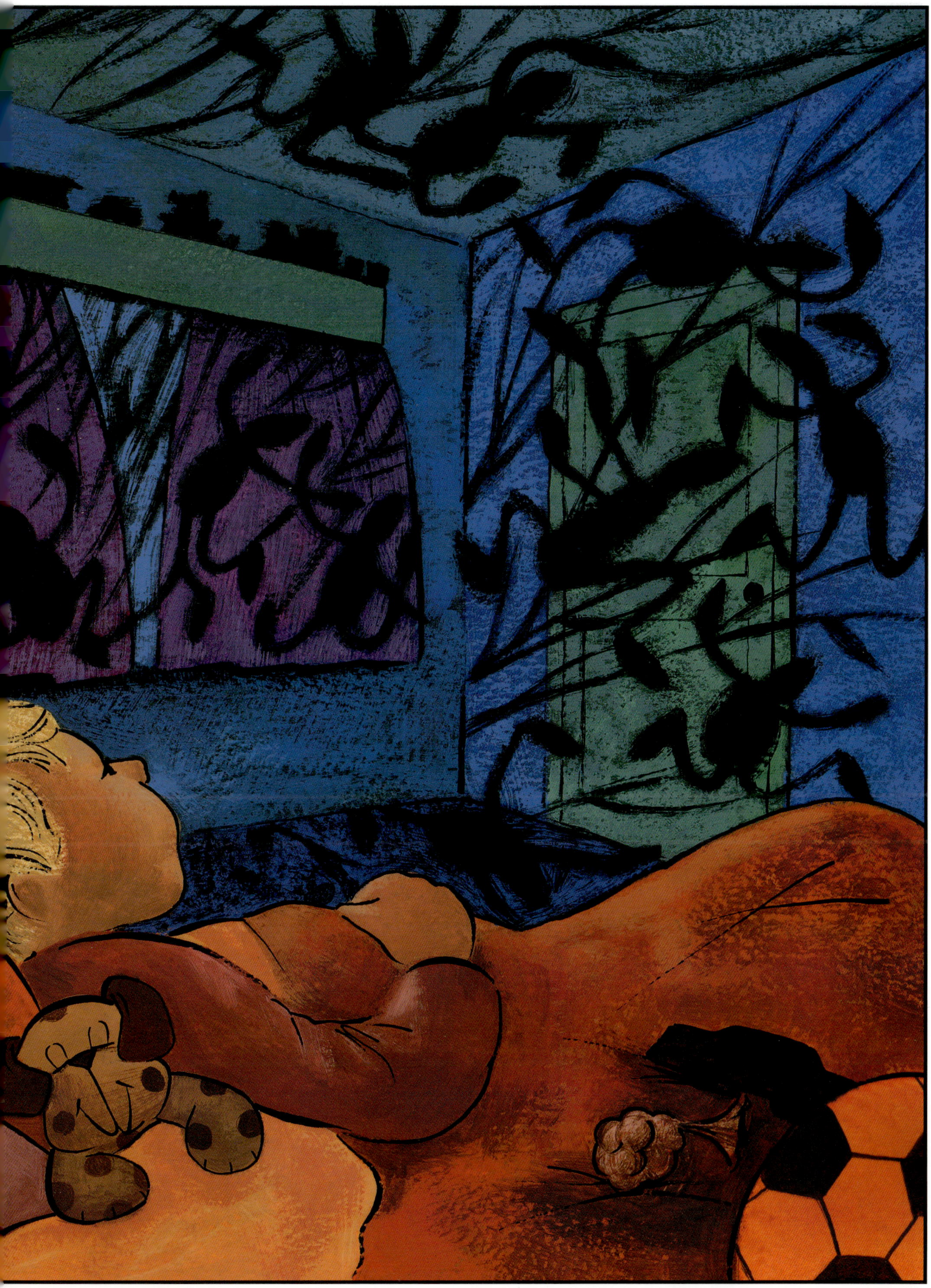

Bird Party

Bird got a letter
and the letter said . . .

Come to a party!
Dress in red!
Wear pink shoes
and a purple hat!
Come to a party,
but don't tell cat!

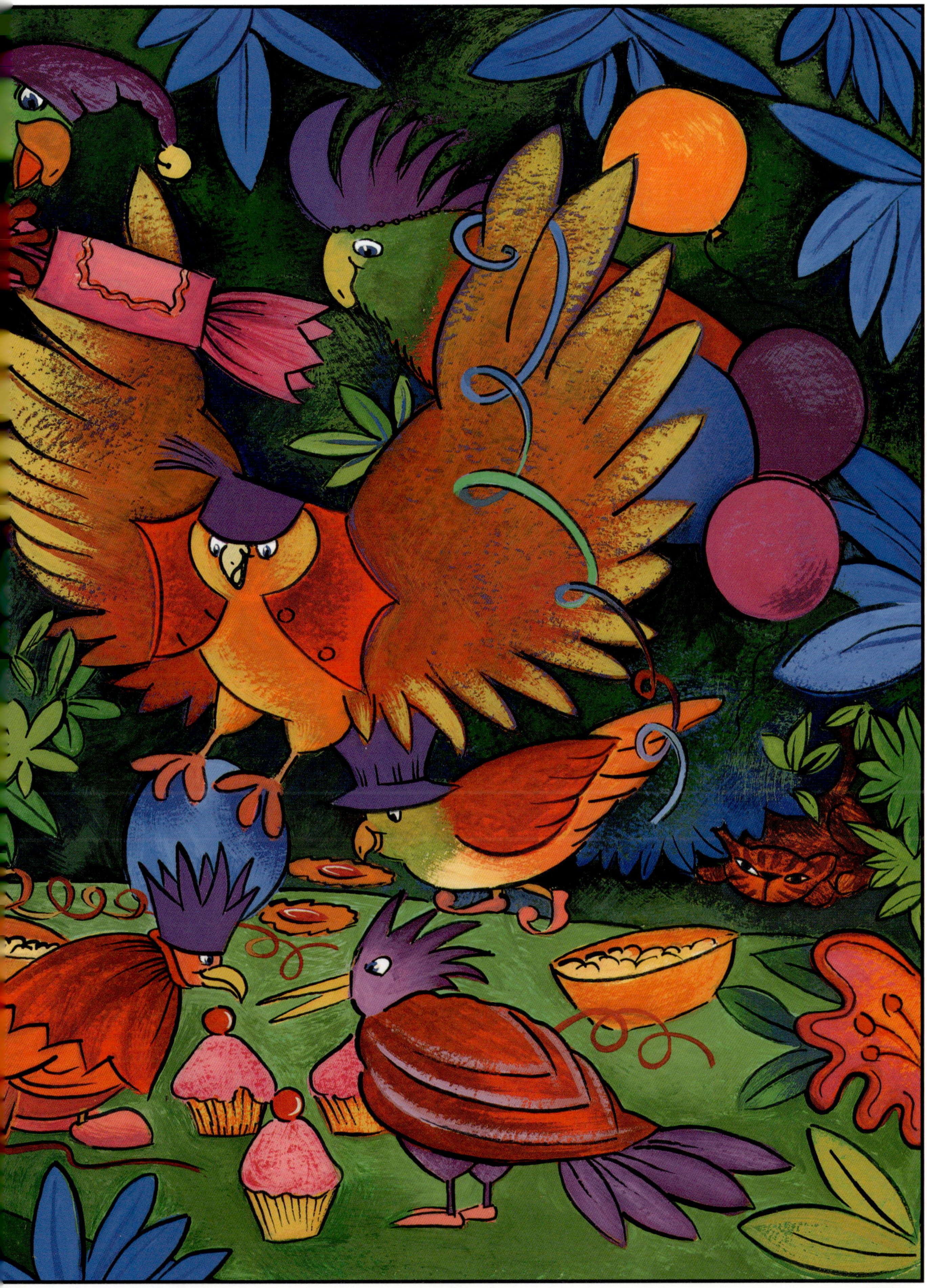

Crocodile Creek

In Crocodile Creek
crocodiles lie,
So...

Don't move your head.
Don't blink your eye.
Don't say a word.
Don't ask why.
Just...

sneak, sneak, sneak
past Crocodile Creek!

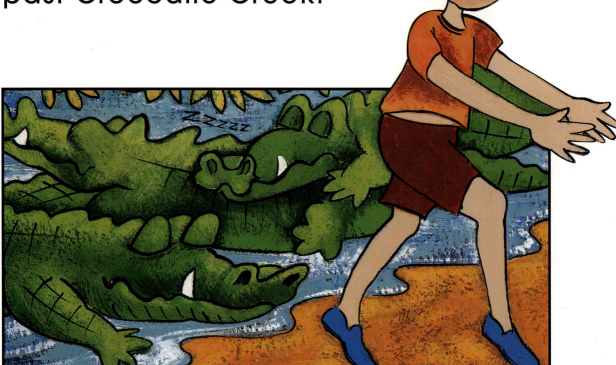